ROME
R. A. STACCIOLI

PAST & PRESENT
WITH RECONSTRUCTIONS

RECONSTRUCTIONS ■   ENTRANCES TO THE ARCHAEOLOGICAL ■
AREAS AND MUSEUMS

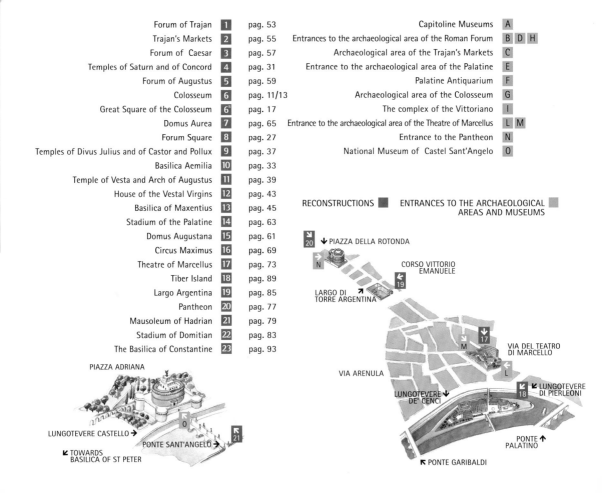

PIAZZA DELLA ROTONDA

CORSO VITTORIO EMANUELE

LARGO DI TORRE ARGENTINA

VIA DEL TEATRO DI MARCELLO

VIA ARENULA

PIAZZA ADRIANA

LUNGOTEVERE CASTELLO →

LUNGOTEVERE DE' CENCI ↓

LUNGOTEVERE DI PIERLEONI

TOWARDS BASILICA OF ST PETER

PONTE SANT'ANGELO →

PONTE PALATINO ↑

PONTE GARIBALDI

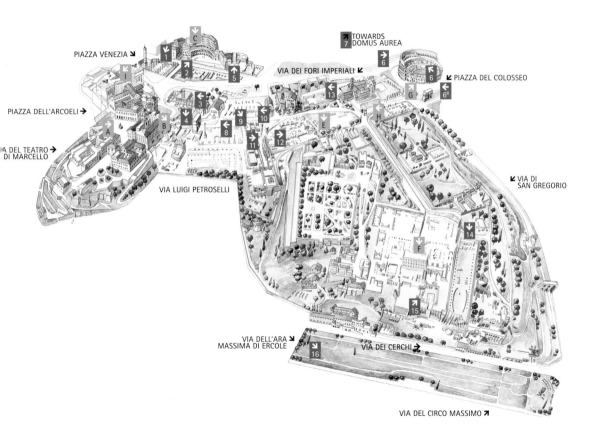

PIAZZA VENEZIA ↘

PIAZZA DELL'ARCOELI →

A DEL TEATRO →
DI MARCELLO

VIA LUIGI PETROSELLI

TOWARDS
DOMUS AUREA

VIA DEI FORI IMPERIALI ↙

PIAZZA DEL COLOSSEO

VIA DI
SAN GREGORIO

VIA DELL'ARA ↘
MASSIMA DI ERCOLE

VIA DEI CERCHI ↗

VIA DEL CIRCO MASSIMO ↗

ROME PAST & PRESENT

INDEX

Text by Romolo Augusto Staccioli

Drawings and reconstructions: (Vision S.r.l.) Tiziana D'Este

Graphic project: Doppiavù studio

Photographs by Vision S.r.l., Spazio Visivo, F. Schneider

I[st] edition 1959
New edition 2008

VISION
ROMA

PAST & PRESENT

Copyright © 2008 VISION S.r.l.

VISION S.r.l. – Via Livorno, 20 – 00162 Roma
Tel/Fax (+39) 06 44292688

e-mail: info@visionpubl.com
www.visionpubl.com

ISBN 978-88-8162-225-2

Printed in Italy by Tipolitografica CS - Padova

THE

From the village of Huts on the Palatine

to the Cosmopolitan City on the banks of the Tiber

MONUMENTS OF ROME

→ *The floors of the two or three huts cut out of the rock of the Palatine and the simple earth graves of a burial ground, the Sepulcretum, on the edge of the Forum are the earliest traces that we can find today of what was later to become Rome, her most ancient 'monuments' as it were. One of the several small villages which had sprang up on these hills separated by broad marshes, the one on the Palatine controlled the Tiber crossing and the market which had long existed on the left bank of the river. This constituted the nucleus around which the other inhabited areas began to concentrate between the 8th and the 7th centuries BC, giving rise over time to the actual city. By the 6th century it was already encircled by walls and protected by a fortified strong point on the Capitoline, it boasted a landing stage on the Tiber and a commercial and political center in the Forum, and it was enriched by public buildings and sanctuaries (most notably the Temple of Jupiter Optimus Maximus Capitolinus).*

View of the northern slopes of the Palatine hill: buildings and shops of ↓ Neronian age and the arches of the Domus Tiberiana.

(→ Over the course of next century the city grew to include the Aventine, and in the first half of the 4th century, following recovery from the invasion of the Gauls and the ruin it had left in its wake, a new circle of walls was erected to protect an extensive urban area, which now covered over 400 hectares. After the conquest of the Greek East (2nd-1st century BC), entire districts were built or redesigned along the lines of eastern cities: Greek architectural models were adopted, such as the public porticus, and new ones were invented, such as the basilica, to house the law courts. The systematic application of arch and vault made it possible to erect ever larger and more functional buildings, such as the commercial porticoes of the vast district known as the Emporium, south of the Aventine. Between 179 and 142 BC, the first stone bridge was built over the Tiber (Pons Aemilius).

The 2nd century also saw a start being made with the building up of the Campus Martius, when the first porticoes and temples were erected; Pompey's projects in the next century (porticoes and a theater) made it the city's natural and most important area of expansion.

↑ Fragment of the *Forma Urbis*, a map of Rome carved on marble slabs under the reign of Septimius Severus: detail showing the theater of Pompeius.

(→ In the 1st century BC, town planning and public building became an explicit part of the political agenda of the heads of state, from Sulla to Pompey and Caesar. The only one of Caesar's grand building projects to survive his death was the construction of a new Forum, the first step in the creation of the monumental complex that the Imperial Fora were later to become. Caesar's successor, Augustus, brought to completion many of the buildings left unfinished (such as the Basilica Julia, the Theater of Marcellus and the Curia). He also built another forum and liberally decorated the Campus Martius with public and private buildings, aided by his helpers, first and foremost among whom was Agrippa: these range from the Theater of Balbus to the Amphitheater of Statilius Taurus, from the Baths of Agrippa to the first Pantheon, and from the Altar of Peace (Ara Pacis) to the Augustan Sundial, and culminate in the grandiose mausoleum erected for the imperial family. And it was also Augustus who, by choosing to live on the Palatine, determined the transformation of the hill into the single magnificent imperial residence of later days. After the terrible fire of 64 AD, which razed to the ground a large part of the city, Nero transformed a good part of the center into a splendid villa, the Domus Aurea (Golden House), and initiated a systematic project for the rebuilding of the city, which can only be said to have been completed under the Flavian dynasty, with Domitian's intense building work and after Vespasian and Titus had, be-

The Ara Pacis dedicated by the Roman Senate to Augustus in the Campus Martius to commemorate the emperor's victories in Spain and in Gaul and the pacifying of the empire (13-9 BC).
↓

Details of one of the marble panels of the Ara Pacis: ↓
The Goddess *Tellus* between the personifications of the *Aurae*, the wind that gives life.

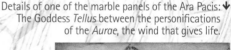

tween 75 and 80, erected the building which would become the symbol of Rome: the Flavian Amphitheater or Colosseum.

The 2nd century AD marked the culmination of Rome's city-planning and building activity. It is to this period that we may trace Trajan's Baths and Forum, the magnificent temples such as that of Venus and Roma, the new Pantheon, the Mausoleum of Hadrian across the Tiber and the two spectacular spiral columns engraved with the exploits of their patrons. Meanwhile in the private sector, multistorey tenements (insulae) were extensively built, often to form genuine neighborhoods.

In the 3rd century there was a general slowing down of activity, notwithstanding the building of the Baths of Caracalla.

In 275 AD Aurelian responded to the growing barbarian menace on the frontiers of the empire by ordering the building of a new circle of city walls, 18km in circumference, which nonetheless contained the great-est, wealthiest and most monumental city yet to be seen on the face of the earth. But building in the city did not come to a complete halt; the Baths of Diocletian and the Basilica of Maxentius, opened by Constantine in 312 AD, constituted two more fantastic chapters in the history of Roman architecture, now spanning back over a thousand years. A little later, the Arch of Constantine, erected in his honour by the Senate in 315 with the recycling of material from older monuments was to mark the end of an era. Indeed, Constantinople, which was to be the empire's new capital, the 'New Rome', was founded on the shores of the Bosphorus on 11 May 330 AD.

← Model of a large apartment building (insula). (Rome, Museo della Civiltà Romana).

ROME
THE COLOSSEUM

General view of Via dei Fori Imperiali and of the valley of the Colosseum. ↑

(→ **The Colosseum**, which in its day was known as the Flavian Amphitheater, was built in the middle of the broad valley between the Palatine, Caelian and Esquiline hills, where Nero had sited the lake in the gardens of his Domus Aurea. As for its imposing size, the figures speak for themselves: the major axis of its elliptical plan is 188m long, the minor axis attains 156m, and the walls in the outer ring rise to almost 50m above ground; more than 100,000 cubic meters of travertine were used to build it and even the metal pins that held the blocks together must have weighed more than 300 tons. Begun by Vespasian shortly after 70 AD, the amphitheater was opened by Titus ten years later.

The ceremonies and games on that occasion went on for a hundred days and some 5000 wild animals were put to death during that time.

The eighty arches at ground level were progressively numbered (the number corresponding to that on the spectator's tessera or admission card) and led, via a system of internal corridors, to the 160 outlets (*vomitoria*) that took the visitor to his place on the steps of the *cavea*, which was borne up by arches and vaults. Beside the amphitheater stood the **Colossus of Nero**, a giant statue of gilt bronze, 30 m high, work of the Greek sculptor Zenodoros. It originally represented the emperor, but after his death was modified to depict the sun god. The interior of the Colosseum consisted of the arena, a wooden floor bearing a bed of sand and covering an area of about 76 m by 46 m, and the stands or *cavea*, subdivided into three superimposed sectors of steps crowned on high by a 'loggia' that housed a fourth order of steps, made of wood and providing the standing room. Each sector of the *cavea* was rigorously reserved for a particular class of citizens, the places on top being assigned to the least important, though all enjoyed free entry.

Counting also the standing spectators, the amphitheater could accommodate about 70,000 people, who came there to watch gladiatorial combats and wild beast hunts as well as less important spectacles of various kinds.
An enormous awning protected the spectators from the heat of the sun; it's segments were hoist-

Coin from Nero's reign with ↑ the emperor's portrait.

The exterior of the Colosseum, → reconstruction.

The interior of the Colosseum, →
reconstruction of the cavea
and of the arena.

ed by a special detachment of sailors sent up from the naval base at Misenum, on the Gulf of Naples.

During shows the arena would be surrounded by a metal mesh carried on poles and spiked with elephant tusks; the top of the mesh was furbished with ivory rollers, so that animals could not get a foothold there and escape from the arena.

Just in case, the niches in the podium at the foot of the steps were always full of archers, ever ready to intervene.

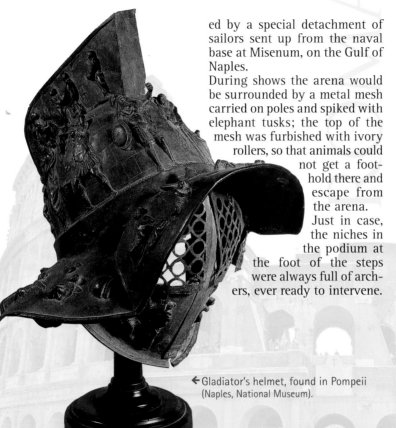

← Gladiator's helmet, found in Pompeii (Naples, National Museum).

The last show of which we have certain knowledge was held in 523 AD under Theodoric, King of the Ostrogoths. It consisted only of animal hunts, for gladiator fighting had been abolished in 438 AD.

A complex system of passages and rooms extended beneath the arena: it was probably constructed under Domitian, after it had been decided that no further 'naval battles' would be staged there. These underground rooms contained facilities and stored the stage equipment for the shows: the scenery was often very elaborate, especially for the hunts, when the stage managers did not fight shy of creating hills, woods, and even small lakes. For men and animals, genuine 'elevators' were made to function, by using counterweights.

THE COLOSSEUM:
UNDERGROUND ROOMS OF THE COLOSSEUM

(➜ The animals, in particular, were first driven along the corridors by their handlers and made to enter cages, which were then raised to a higher level, where the cage would open. The animals could thus step out onto a gangway connected to a ramp, with a trap door at its upper end, from which they would exit into the open, ready for the show.

We are told that on one occasion this system was used to bring a hundred lions into the arena at one and the same moment: their combined roar was so loud that the noisy crowd was frightened into instant silence.

The gladiators were able to reach the arena direct from their main 'barracks' (*Ludus Magnus*), situated by the side of the Colosseum, by using an underground passage leading to the amphitheater's underground spaces.

↓ Relief showing duelling scenes between gladiators
(Chieti, funerary monument of C. Lusius Storax).

THE GREAT SQUARE
OF THE COLOSSEUM

(➔ Overshadowed by the immense mass of the amphitheater, the **great square of the Colosseum** assumed its final monumental appearance with the building of the **Temple of Venus and Rome**, and this layout has been substantially preserved right down to our own day. Ordained and possibly also designed by Hadrian, this temple, dedicated to the divine ancestress of the Julian family and to the city, mistress of the world, was inaugurated in 135 AD and then reconstructed by

← The Arch of Constantine.

Square of the Colosseum: the *Meta* ➔ *Sudans* in the middle, the Colossus of Nero on the right, the Temple of Venus and Rome in the background.

Maxentius round about 310 AD, after it had been destroyed by fire. It had two apses, standing back to back at the center of a broad terrace on the Velian hill (which at that time stretched beyond today's Via dei Fori Imperiali, from the Palatine hill towards the Esquiline) and was

Round relief from the eastern side of ↓ the Arch of Constantine representing the Sun god on his four-horse chariot rising from the sea.

surrounded on at least two sides by porticoes.

The remains of the 'vestibule' of Nero's Golden House were torn down to make room for this temple and even the Colossus of Nero had to be shifted. Twelve pairs of elephants were used to move it.

At the beginning of the road which leaves the Square of the Colosseum to run down into the Forum, there was a fountain built in the middle of the 1st century AD, which had a shape rather like one of the *metae* or

← Colossal portrait of emperor Constantine (Rome, Capitoline Museum).

← Relief of the eastern side of the Arch of Constantine representing the procession of the triumphant Constantine entering Rome.

Detail of the columns → of the Temple of Venus and Rome.

turning points in the Circus that the chariots had to race round: it therefore came to be known as *Meta Sudans*, the Turn of Sweat.

The last monument added to adorn this great square was the **Arch of Constantine**. As its inscription records, it was erected in 312 AD by the Senate and People of Rome in honour of the Emperor, who had liberated the city and the state from the 'tyrant' Maxentius by his victory in the battle of the Milvian Bridge. The arch was richly decorated with sculpture taken from earlier monuments erected by Trajan, Hadrian and Marcus Aurelius in the 2nd century, and only the small reliefs which run round the whole monument actually depict events in which Constantine himself was involved.

Arch of Constantine: statue of a Dacian warrior. →

Arch of Constantine, battle ➔
of the emperor Trajan
against the Dacians.

← The Temple of Venus
and Rome seen from the
Square of the Colosseum.

(→ The Roman Forum was the commercial, religious, political and legal center of the city, at any rate throughout the Republic, and remained a sacred and monumental area throughout antiquity. Its origins are related the coalescing into a city of the primitive villages which had grown up on the higher parts of the surrounding hills.

The **valley of the Forum**, lying between the Palatine, the Capitol and the first slopes of the Viminal and the Quirinal, must itself have been affected, albeit marginally, by the presence of some modest nuclei of huts and by an extensive burial ground, dating back to the late bronze age and the early iron age. Around about the end of the 7th century BC, the *Cloaca Maxima* drained away its stagnant waters and it could thus be formally laid out and receive its first 'paving'.

↓ The Roman Forum, at night: in the foreground the Temple of Saturn.

THE ROMAN FORUM

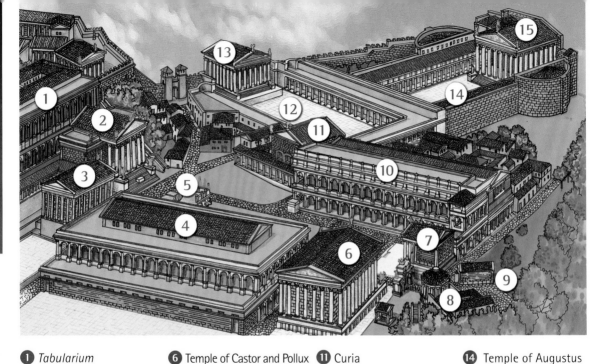

1 *Tabularium*
2 Temple of Concord
3 Temple of Saturn
4 Basilica Julia
5 *Rostra*

6 Temple of Castor and Pollux
7 Temple of Divus Julius
8 Temple of Vesta
9 *Regia*
10 Basilica Aemilia

11 Curia
12 The Forum of Caesar
13 Temple of Venus Genetrix

14 Temple of Augustus
15 Temple of Mars Ultor

THE ROMAN FORUM
AT THE TIME OF AUGUSTUS

(➜ From that time onwards, the part of the valley lying at the foot of the Capitol was set aside for political functions (with the construction of the **Curia**, for the meetings of the Senate, and the **Comitium**, for the assemblies of the people), while the remainder, much larger, came to play the part of the 'square' (the Forum in the proper sense of the term), where shops and market stalls intermingled with the city's oldest sanctuaries, of **Vesta, Saturn, Janus** and **Castor and Pollux**.

The Roman Forum: the Curia building. ➜

(➜ A small sanctuary consisting of an altar, an honorary column and a tufa block with an inscription dating back to the 6th century BC was interpreted as being the grave of the legendary founder, Romulus, and protected with big slabs of black stone (*Lapis Niger*).

The *Via Sacra* crossed the whole length of the square, whence it ascended to the Temple of Jupiter Optimus Maximus on the Capitol.

← The Roman Forum: the *Lapis Niger*.

(→ The construction of the first **Basilicas** during the 2nd century BC (the *Porcia*, the oldest, the *Opimia*, the *Sempronia*, and most importantly the *Basilica Aemilia*) further emphasized the Forum's character as a political and administrative center, and it gradually assumed its definitive appearance.

■ ■ ■

The stages in this process were: the building of the *Tabularium*, seat of the state archives on the slopes of the Capitol (80 BC), providing the square with a monumental backdrop; the moving of the Curia and the *Rostra* (the platform from which the magistrates addressed the people) and the erection of the **Basilica Julia** in front of the Basilica Aemilia by Caesar, marking off the long sides of the square; and finally, the positioning of the Temple of Divus Julius, ordained by Augustus, in order to close off the fourth side of the square.

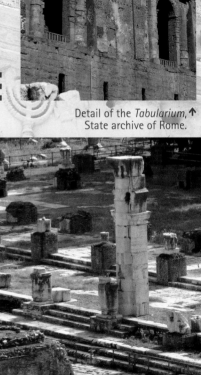

Detail of the *Tabularium*, ↑
State archive of Rome.

Roman Forum: The Basilica Julia. ↓

← Roman Forum, the Temple of Antoninus and Faustina.

(→ The structure of the square remained unchanged for a long time. The construction of new buildings, such as the **Temple of Vespasian and Titus** and that of **Antoninus and Faustina**, built by Antoninus Pius in memory of his wife Faustina, who died in 141 BC, and subsequently dedicated by the Senate to the emperor himself, respected the Augustan layout.

The only breach in this convention was the erection of a gigantic equestrian statue of Domitian in the center of the square.

Only from the 3rd century AD onwards was the Forum area once again invaded by commemorative and honorary monuments: the **Arch of Septimius Severus**, squeezed in between the *Rostra* and the Curia, the **seven honorary columns** lined up along the south side of the square, in front of the Basilica Julia, and the monuments commemorating the tenth anniversary (*decennalia*) of the Tetrarchy.

Indeed, it fell to one of these columns, the one raised in 608 AD in honour of the Byzantine emperor Phocas, to become the last monument to be added to the Forum. But by that time the millenary glory of what had once been the most important place in Rome had long since faded away.

Plautus, in his comedy *Curculio*, has left us a very vivid and fascinating picture of life in the Forum under the Republic, revealing the characteristics of each

↑ Equestrian statue of the emperor Marcus Aurelius (Rome, Capitoline Museum).

place, according to the people frequenting it: 'There in the Comitium, where the judges sit and the orators make their speeches from the platform, you can see the perjurers, the liars and the braggarts; down there in the square near the statue of Marsyas, are the advocates, the litigants and the witnesses; beside the shops, old and new, in front of the basilica are the strumpets, the bankers, the usurers and the brokers; in the lowest part of the Forum, the serious-minded and the gentlemen who conduct themselves quietly; in the middle, near the canal, the good-for-nothings (*canalicolae*), parasites waiting for a tip from the rich and drunkards; higher up are the gossips and scandalmongers. Behind the Temple of Castor and the Vicus Tuscus, the criminals and the men of bad fame collect; in the Velabrum are the bakers, butchers, fortune-tellers and dancers; beside the Fountain of Juturna the sick, who drink the miraculous waters; nearby, in the fish market, the bonviveurs. Everywhere the rabble of the idle vagabonds, the men about town – the type that are either deep in gaming or spreading false rumors and passing pompous judgments on affairs of state...'

← The Roman Forum: the honorary column raised in honour of emperor Phocas in 608 AD.

The Square of the Roman Forum, reconstruction. →

(→ But alongside this teeming everyday life in the Forum there was always also another, more or less official life of public affairs and activities. It was here that the magistrates had their official seats and offices; the Consuls and the Senators in the Curia, the Tribunes in the Comitium, the Praetors in the courts; it was from the platform of the *Rostra* that magistrates and candidates for a political career harangued the crowd; and it was in the Comitium that the people elected their magistrates, and in the Curia that the Senators met. Religious processions and sacrifices to the gods took place here, as did the grand funerals, sometimes stopping before the *Rostra*, from which laudatory speeches were made in honour of the dead (among them the most famous of all: Mark Antony's speech in honour of Caesar). The gladiatorial shows offered free of charge to the people also took place in the square prior to the building of the amphitheaters. Especially famous among these is the fight organized by Caesar as *aedilis* in 65 BC, when no less than 320 pairs of gladiators took part. Just as famous was the banquet that Caesar gave on the occasion of his triumph in 45 BC, which lasted for several days and catered for 22,000 guests.

↑ Arch of Titus: the spoils from the temple at Jerusalem.

← The Arch of Titus, built to celebrate the triumph of the emperor for the conquest of Jerusalem.

THE TEMPLES OF SATURN AND CONCORD

(→ Tradition has it that the **Temple of Saturn** was begun during the last years of the kings and inaugurated at the beginning of the Republic (498/7 AD) and it was venerated as one of the most ancient shrines of Rome. But its appearance today is that given it by a restoration late in the 3rd century AD made necessary by an outbreak of fire. Its huge base encloses a space that was intended for use as the State Treasury, the *Aerarium.* At the foot of the staircase leading up to the temple entrance, Augustus, in 20 BC, set up a tall column (the *Miliarum Aureum*) on which were inscribed, in letters of gilt bronze, the distances from Rome to the principal cities of the Empire. At the column, which was considered as the center (*umbilicus*) of Rome, there commenced the *Clivus Capitolinus*, which was an extension of the Via Sacra and climbed the Capitol right up to the Temple of Jupiter, passing in front of the **Temple of Vespasian and Titus**, which was begun by Titus in honour of his deified father and completed by his brother and successor, Domitian. Another building along the Clivus was the **Portico of the Consenting Gods** (*Dei Consentes*), which housed gilt bronze statues of the twelve Olympian gods grouped in pairs according to the classical tradition.

← The Roman Forum: Temple of Saturn.

(→ Next to the Temple of Vespasian there stood the **Temple of Concord,** which was likewise built up against the *Tabularium*, or state archives. This temple was attributed to Marcus Furius Camillus, who was said to have had it built in 367 BC to commemorate the peace settlement achieved that year by Patricians and Plebeians. Frequently repaired and eventually completely reconstructed by Tiberius, this temple has the distinctive feature of a *cella* arranged in the longitudinal direction.

Ancient authors often noted the fact that the many pictures and statues by famous artists kept in this temple had turned it into a museum. On this side, directly facing the square, was **the platform of the *Rostra*,** decorated with the bronze prows taken from the ships of the Volscians at

the end of the 4th century BC. Opposite the Temple of Concord stood the **Arch of Septimius Severus,** which was erected by the Senate and People of Rome in 202 AD to commemorate the emperor, who had extended the boundaries of the Empire as far as Mesopotamia.

The Temples of Saturn and of Concord, reconstruction. →

THE BASILICA AEMILIA

Reconstruction of the Basilica Aemilia's façade. →

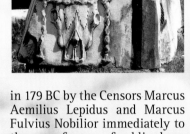

Basilica Aemilia, relief with → a *bucranium* (ox-skull).

(→ Facing directly onto the Forum, **the Basilica Aemilia,** sole survivor of the Republican basilicas, delimited its northern side, together with the Curia building on the other side of the ancient road known as the Argiletum. Beyond the Curia, the *Tullianum*, or 'Mamertine' Prison, lay at the foot of the mass of the Arx Capitolina, the view of which was partially obscured by the Arch of Septimius Severus and crowned by the Temple of Juno Moneta.

The purpose of Basilica Aemilia was to provide visitors to the Forum with a comfortable and sheltered place where, during the winter and also in case of bad weather in summer, it would be possible to carry out at least some of the functions that normally took place in the open, especially those connected with the administration of justice and business in general.

The Basilica was actually built in 179 BC by the Censors Marcus Aemilius Lepidus and Marcus Fulvius Nobilior immediately to the rear of a row of public shops (*tabernae*) intended for use by bankers. Subsequently modified on many occasions (lastly by Augustus in 14 BC and by Tiberius in 22 AD), it ended up by

Basilica Aemilia, frieze showing → Rome's origins.

32

ROME THE ROMAN FORUM

Basilica Aemilia, entrance arch. ↑

Basilica Aemilia, the remains ↓
of the central nave.

incorporating these shops in its ground floor portico, which consisted of a series of sixteen arches spanning between pilasters with half-engaged columns, and supported another similar portico on the upper floor.

The interior of the basilica consisted of four aisles with intervening rows of columns, and during the reign of Augustus it received a splendid marble floor. This marble still preserves traces of the fire that destroyed the basilica in 410 AD during the sack of the city by the Visigoths under Alaric. In front of its steps, a small round *sacellum* was dedicated to Cloacina, divinity of the Cloaca Maxima, which runs right underneath. It is said that it marks the point where the Romans and the Sabines made peace and purified themselves after the battle fought in the Forum following the famous 'rape' of the Sabine women.

THE TEMPLES OF DIVUS JULIUS AND OF CASTOR AND POLLUX

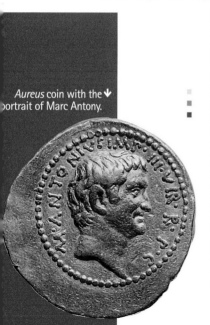

Aureus coin with the ↓ portrait of Marc Antony.

(→ After the murder of Caesar on 15 March 44 BC, the Senate at once decreed solemn honors to the dictator's memory and erected an altar and honorary column on the site where his body had been cremated. It was not until 31 BC, however, that Octavian, Caesar's adoptive son and heir, began to build a temple there, which was completed two years later, in 29, and dedicated to **Divus Julius**, the Deified Caesar. An interesting detail is the recess built into the front of the podium to accommodate the existing altar, which was then walled in to gain the space for an orators' platform above it. This platform, the New *Rostra*, was adorned with the bronze rams taken from the ships of Antony and Cleopatra after the battle of Actium. The temple was flanked by two arches, one on the south side in memory of the Battle of Actium, the other, on the opposite side, ordained by the Senate to celebrate the restitution to the emperor Augustus of the Legionary Standards, captured from the Triumvir Crassus by the Parthians during the battle of Carrhae. It is possible that this was later dedicated to his two nephews and heirs, the princes Gaius and Lucius Caesar.

Next to Caesar's temple there stood the **Temple of Castor and Pollux**, which had occupied this position ever since the early part of the 5th century BC.

The Temple of Divus Julius: the so-called *ara* of Caesar, remains of an altar ↑ probably raised on the spot where the dictator's body was cremated.

THE TEMPLES OF DIVUS JULIUS AND OF CASTOR AND POLLUX

(→ Legend attributes its construction to a war fought against Etruscans and Latins, when two youths of extraordinary beauty and stature were seen riding, lance in rest, at the head of the Roman cavalry, leading it to victory. Almost at the same moment two identical youths were seen in the Forum, dismounting from sweating horses and leading them to drink at the Fountain of Juturna; to those who asked them for news of the battle, they told how the Romans had won the day.

Then they vanished, and all who had seen them were ready to swear that they were none other than the Dioscuri, Castor and Pollux, the sons of Jupiter. Aulus Postumius Albinus, who was in command of the cavalry on the day of this portentous vision (15 July 499 BC), therefore vowed a temple to the twin demigods, and it was opened by his son fifteen years later. Over the years it was frequent-ly restored and enlarged, the last time in the 6th century AD, when the young Tiberius gave in its final form, to which belong the three columns that are still standing. Built into its base were several shops housing the activities of jewelers, money changers, and even barbers.

← Marble portrait of queen Cleopatra.

The Temple of Divus Julius and, → to the right, the Temple of Castor and Pollux, reconstruction.

THE TEMPLE OF VESTA AND THE ARCH OF AUGUSTUS

Detail of the Temple of Vesta. ➜

The Temple of Vesta, ➜
the Arch of Augustus and
the Temple of Castor and Pollux; in
the background the Palatine.

(➜ At the point in the Forum, where the ground begins to rise towards the slopes of the Palatine, there stood a temple that was of the utmost importance for the city and her population, for it was dedicated to the goddess who was protectress of the family and thus also of the State: the **Temple of Vesta**, traditionally attributed to Numa Pompilius, one of the first kings of Rome. Within it the Vestal Virgins guarded the sacred and eternal flame, symbol of the eternal life of the city. Stored away in the innermost shrine of this temple and equally jealously guarded, the city also preserved numerous sacred objects, including the Palladium, the wooden image of Pal-

las Athena, that, as legend would have it, Aeneas had brought from Troy as pledge and warranty of empire. According to some authors, this temple was round in plan because it had originally been built on the model of a hut, the oldest type of hearth and home known in Italy, and had an opening in the roof to let out the smoke generated by the fire. It was frequently rebuilt following destruction by fire, the last time at the end of the 2nd century AD by Julia Domna, wife of the emperor Septimius Severus. Opposite the Temple of Vesta, astride the *Vicus Vestae* just before it joins the Via Sacra, rose the **Arch of Augustus**, and right in front of this, a small fountain with a circular basin made of white marble.

The triple arch was erected by the Senate to commemorate Octavian's victory over Antony and Cleopatra at Actium, in 31 BC. Its middle passageway was vaulted. It is believed that the lists of con-

Golden coin with the portrait ↑ of the emperor Augustus.

suls and records of all those generals who had obtained the honour of a triumph since the beginning of the Republic (*Fasti*) were engraved on special marble panels on the inner walls of the arch.

At the back, behind the imposing mass of the **Temple of Castor and Pollux** which stood over the Arch, were the buildings of the Imperial Palaces on the Palatine, which faced onto the Forum.

Head of a Vestal Virgin (*Antiquarium* of the Palatine).

The **House of the Vestal Virgins**, which rose immediately adjacent to the Temple of Vesta, was the home and official residence of the priestesses charged with guarding the sacred fire that burned in the temple and performing the rites connected with the cult of the hearth. The Vestal Virgins were six in number; they entered as novices between the age of six and ten, and remained for thirty years under vows of strict chastity. They were chosen by the supreme religious authority of the State, the *Pontifex Maximus*; at first only Patricians were eligible, but later they could be chosen also from among the Plebeian families.

The Vestal Virgins received a rich dowry from the State, and they were allotted every honour, including that of being accompanied by lictors, a privilege they shared with the consuls.

THE HOUSE OF THE VESTAL VIRGINS

The House of the Vestal Virgins → seen from the Palatine hill.

(→ Such was their sacred dignity that if by chance a condemned criminal happened to cross their path, he was automatically reprieved. But they also lived under the menace of a tremendous punishment, for any priestess who allowed the fire to go out or became untrue to her vow of chastity would be buried alive (with a loaf of bread and a lamp) in a small underground chamber in the 'field of the wicked' (*Campus Sceleratus*) just outside the walls on the Quirinal. The House, which has been considered as the prototype of present-day monastic convents, was organized around a large courtyard kept as a garden and surrounded on all sides by a portico. All of the rooms opened onto these galleries, which also gave access to the other spaces of the house, including the quarters of the servants. Self-sufficient in every respect, the house was well appointed and one can still recognize the kitchen, the flour mill, and the ovens. The private rooms were situated on the upper floor, complete with baths and heating facilities, while one of the long sides on the ground floor included a *sacellum* dedicated to the tutelary gods (*Lares*); it was flanked by three rooms on either side, the offices of the six Vestal Virgins. The large room on the opposite side, is thought to have been a *triclinium*.

The building of irregular form located to the south of the House of the Vestals was the Royal Palace (*Regia*), traditionally thought to have been the residence of King Numa, seat of the *Pontifex Maximus* until Augustus donated it to the Vestals.

In front of the House of the Vestals on the other side of the Via Sacra is an imposing monument, consist-

ing of a round central part topped by a dome, with a concave facade containing four niches for the housing of statues and two lateral sections projecting forward on either side. The portal is flanked by two porphyry columns with capitals in white marble. The large bronze door is original, still perfectly preserved. The building is commonly identified as the **Temple of Divus Romulus**, the son of Maxentius, who died young in 307 BC and was deified. It is, however, very likely that a new identification must be ascribed, though this is still the subject of debate, and it is probably the reworking of a previous temple.

← The great bronze door of the Temple of Divus Romulus.

THE BASILICA OF MAXENTIUS

← Portrait statue of
the emperor Maxentius.

(→ The emperor Maxentius never saw his **Basilica** finished. He died on the banks of the Tiber at the Milvian Bridge after the famous battle against Constantine in 312 AD. So it was Constantine who inaugurated the last and biggest of the Roman basilicas, after incorporating a few changes of his own.

The edifice, one of Imperial Rome's most grandiose, occupied most of the Velia, overlooking the Forum from the east. The basilica covers an area of 100m x 65m, and rests on a large artificial platform built into the side of the hill in the place formerly occupied by the triple portico which had served as the vestibule of Nero's Golden House and was later converted into warehouses and shops for luxury goods and rarities imported from the East. It contained a large central nave terminating in an apse on the west side, flanked by two smaller aisles. These were not roofed by means of beams laid horizontally on the columns, but by cross vaults springing from pilasters in the manner that had by then been in use for over a century in the great 'basilicas' of the bath buildings. This made it possible for the central part of the building to rise to a height of 35 m above the floor; the extraordinary simplicity with which this result was obtained, together with the extreme clarity of spaces, right up to the patterning of the

The Basilica of Maxentius, reconstruction of the interior. →

coffering on the ceiling, conferred upon the interior a wonderful sense of harmony.

A colossal statue of Constantine in marble and gilt bronze occupied the west apse.

At the end of the 4th century AD, a grand new entrance was opened onto the Via Sacra on the south side, and the addition of a deep apse with niches in the central arcade of the right aisle altered the orientation of the basilica, now perpendicular to its previous axis.

This magnificent roof fell in 1349 as the result of an earthquake. Just one of the eight columns (20 m high) forming part of the pilasters remained in its original position until 1614, when Pope Paul V removed it (using sixty horses for the purpose) to the square of Santa Maria Maggiore.

THE IMPERIAL FORA

(→ The splendid group of monuments that constitute the **Imperial Fora** originally came into being to meet the need for more space than was available in the old political and administrative center, as the population of the city multiplied and the amount of business to be transacted increased. The process began towards the end of the Republican period in the 1st century BC. Caesar was the first to think of enlarging the time-honored square of the Roman Forum by building a new Forum immediately adjacent to it and at the very foot of the citadel (*Arx*) on the Capitol; this forum later became known by the dictator's name (*Forum Julium*). It had the absolutely regular form of an elongated rectangle, all planned on the model of the public squares (*agorai*) of Hellenistic cities, with porticoes and shops on three sides and a temple in the center.

Following the example of his adoptive father, Augustus, some fifty years later, built another Forum of practically the same size somewhat to the east, between the Forum of Caesar and the Quirinal. His

THE ROMAN FORUM
AND THE IMPERIAL FORA

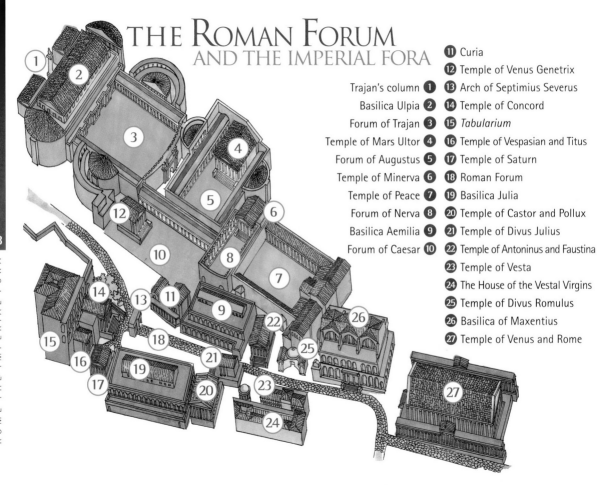

Trajan's column **1**
Basilica Ulpia **2**
Forum of Trajan **3**
Temple of Mars Ultor **4**
Forum of Augustus **5**
Temple of Minerva **6**
Temple of Peace **7**
Forum of Nerva **8**
Basilica Aemilia **9**
Forum of Caesar **10**

11 Curia
12 Temple of Venus Genetrix
13 Arch of Septimius Severus
14 Temple of Concord
15 *Tabularium*
16 Temple of Vespasian and Titus
17 Temple of Saturn
18 Roman Forum
19 Basilica Julia
20 Temple of Castor and Pollux
21 Temple of Divus Julius
22 Temple of Antoninus and Faustina
23 Temple of Vesta
24 The House of the Vestal Virgins
25 Temple of Divus Romulus
26 Basilica of Maxentius
27 Temple of Venus and Rome

forum was separated from the ill-famed district of the Suburra by a high stone wall that also served to protect it from the violent fires that frequently ravaged the Suburra. The only novelty introduced by the **Forum of Augustus** was constituted by the fact that its sides were bounded by two large covered hemicycles fronted by porticoes with a double order of columns and decorated internally by engaged columns and niches containing statues.

With the two new Fora of Caesar and Augustus Rome's center had become adequate in size to meet her needs, all the more so when, immediately after his triumph in the Jewish War, the emperor Vespasian constructed a **Temple of Peace** in the vicinity of the Forum of Augustus, using it to display the booty taken from the Temple at Jerusalem. By the time he had surrounded it with gardens and a three-sided portico, he had in effect built a new forum, though it was not officially called so until much later.

When Domitian, subsequently, used the space left free between the Forum of Augustus and the Temple of Peace to construct yet another forum (known as the **Forum of Nerva**, who inaugurated it in 97 AD, or, more popularly, as the '*Transitorium*', on account of its leading from one into the other), he had not only solved all problems of layout and direct communications, but had also brought to life a unique

Forum Transitorium, south-eastern wall: «le Colonnacce». ↓

■ ■ ■ buildings and monuments of a certain value. But this forum served to put the administrative center and the old city into direct communication with the 'new' city that had grown up in the Campus Martius area, thus realizing a dream already cherished by Augustus.

The Forum of Trajan was the last of the Imperial Fora, but it was also the most grandiose and resplendent of them all. 300m long and 185m wide, it also included the Basilica Ulpia, so called after one of the emperor's other names, libraries and a magnificent honorary column. An inscription placed at the base of the column is still legible, informing us that the column's height, of about 40 meters, corresponds to the height of the hill which was leveled at that point.

and continuous complex, well worthy of being the center of the sovereign city of the world.

↑
Frieze with Victories from the main nave of the Basilica Ulpia.

(→ This did not deter Trajan (98-117 AD) from adding the forum that now bears his name, entrusting its construction to Apollodorus, a famous Damascan architect. In order to create it, the high ground that joined the Capitol to the Quirinal and entire streets of houses were swept away, including some

THE FORUM OF TRAJAN

(→ It is possible that the work of clearing away the hill to make room for the new forum was begun by Domitian, but Trajan alone was responsible for building the whole of the immense complex. He inaugurated the forum in 112 and the column in 113. The whole building was a hymn to the triumph of the emperor over the Dacian barbarians, people inhabiting the area of what is now Romania.

The enormous square, with its equestrian statue of the emperor in the middle, was sealed off to the east by the basilica, and surrounded by porticoes on the other sides, of which the western one was curved. The porticoes on the long sides bore an attic storey decorated with statues of barbarians alternating with reliefs depicting piles of captured arms and portraits of previous emperors and members of the imperial family (*imagines clipeatae*). In the middle of each long side was a deep exedra, separated from the porticus by a row of columns. The facade of the great basilica overlooking the square contained a columnar porch stepped forward in three parts, each surmounted by bronze groups with two-horse or four-horse chariots. The interior consisted of a double-aisled, double-storeyed porticus which went around the sides of a huge central hall. On the short sides, beyond the porticus, there were two exedras, symmetrical to the ones in the forum, which were used as courts of justice.

Detail of Trajan's Column. →

(→ The west side of the basilica looked onto a small courtyard, at the center of which rose the column with its pictorial narrative, while the north and south sides were occupied by the two libraries, one Greek and one Latin.

The column shaft is completely decorated with figures illustrating the exploits of the emperor during the conquest of Dacia.

Visitors to the forum were able to admire the reliefs of the column and follow the account from the terraces of the libraries and basilica.

After the emperor's death and deification, the complex housed his ashes in a massive gold urn placed inside the base of the column, and it celebrated his divinity with the construction of a great temple which recent research suggests was locat-ed in the middle of the curved eastern side. A story told by the historian Ammianus Marcellinus bears witness to the magnificence of the entire complex even in late antiquity: when the eastern emperor Constantius II arrived in Rome for the first time in 356 AD, so struck was he by the beauty of the equestrian statue of Trajan, rising in the middle of the forum square, that he expressed a desire to have one like it made of himself; at which his companion, the Persian prince Hormisdas, quipped: «But first, my lord, have a stable built to match this one, if you can.

Then, by all means, tell them to make the horse which you intend to erect in the likeness of the one before us».

Trajan's Forum, drawing →
reconstructing the Basilica Ulpia.

← Trajan's Column, frieze.

TRAJAN'S MARKETS

Central hall of Trajan's Markets and → section of the Basilica Ulpia, reconstruction.

(→ The enormous, brick-faced complex known today as «Trajan's Markets», actually composed of distinct parts, completely covers and contains the rock face laid bare with the removal of the saddle which connected the Capitol to the Quirinal, a vast operation of urban redesign undertaken in order to obtain the flat area occupied by the Forum of Trajan.

The building is divided into various parts. The lowest consists of a broad hemicycle following the curve of the exedra of the Forum of Trajan, facing onto the street with a series of small interiors probably used for commercial purposes (*tabernae*). At either end there are two apsidal halls.

Three storeys high, the hemicycle reaches the level of a second paved street still known by its Medieval name: the *Via Biberatica*. Above this street extend the complex's other two nuclei: a large cross-vaulted hall with three storeys of rooms on each side and, further east, a complex of rooms with niches in the walls, arranged around a large domed hall and around a light well.

It is thought that this was the headquarters of the imperial official (*procurator*) responsible for the management of the Forum of Trajan.

Indeed, inscriptions uncovered during the most recent excavations show that the whole complex of «markets» housed the offices of the forum administration, so that the actual forum area could be devoted entirely to the functions for which it was designed, i.e. those of celebration and display.

THE FORUM OF CAESAR

(→ When Caesar decided to construct a new forum beside the old, there were serious problems that had to be solved before his plan could be executed. Apart from purchasing and demolishing the numerous houses that occupied the chosen area, a great deal of earth had to be removed to level the site, a long stairway had to be cut in the slope of the Capitol, and the neighboring Senate House had to be moved, together with all its accessory buildings. The enormous cost of all this (the sole purchase of the land called for a hundred million *sestertii*) was met out of the vast spoils of the Gallic Wars. Particular care was paid to the design and construction of the most important monument in this Forum, the **Temple** dedicated to **Venus Genetrix**, which Caesar himself had vowed to erect on the eve of the Battle of Pharsalus against his rival Pompey.

Venus was considered to be the divine progenitrix of the family to which Caesar belonged, for she was said to be the mother of Aeneas, the Trojan hero, who – after his flight from the burning city and many years of wandering over the Mediterranean – settled at last in Latium at the mouth of the Tiber. There, before he could marry Lavinia the daughter of the king of Latium, he had to fight a final battle against the king of Ardea, Turnus. But Aeneas won and he and Lavinia had a son, Iulus, who was said to be the ancestor of the Julians. The temple was inaugurated on 26 September in the year 46 BC, and Caesar adorned it with numerous works of art, including two pictures by Thymomachus of Byzantium, which he had bought for 80 talents, six collections of engraved gems and a jeweled cuirass he had taken in Britain. The temple also contained a statue of Caesar and another of Cleopatra. As regards the cult statue itself, it was the work of the Greek sculptor Archesilaos and showed Venus with a cupid on her shoulders and holding a child in her arms. It stood in the apse which opened in the rear wall of the temple's cell.

← Basalt bust of Gaius Julius Caesar (Berlin, Staatmuseum).

Caesar's Forum and the Temple → of Venus Genetrix.

THE FORUM OF AUGUSTUS

(→ Augustus took his decision to build a new forum by means of a vow he made to Mars before the Battle of Philippi (42 BC), in which he defeated Brutus and Cassius, the murderers of Caesar. Nevertheless, the **Temple of Mars Ultor** (i.e. Mars the Avenger), the very centerpiece of the Forum, was not inaugurated until forty years later. Built entirely of Carrara marble, this temple had eight columns on the facade and a like number on both sides, while its pediment was decorated by a high relief which had as its central figure Mars leaning on his lance and standing between Venus (with Eros) and Fortuna; further to the right there was the Goddess Roma and a figure representing the River Tiber, while to the left of Venus one could see Romulus in the act of taking the omen from a flight of birds, followed by a personalization of the Palatine.

Caesar's sword was kept in the cell of this temple, together with the legionary standards which had been lost to the Parthians in the defeat of Crassus, Augustus having succeeded in getting them back. This forum was dedicated to exalting the emperor and his role as preserver of tradition and embodiment of the city's historical destiny, within a 'providential' design that the gods both desired and protected. A large number of statues of heroes (Aeneas and his son Iulus, Romulus, the kings of Albalonga) and great historical figures (*summi viri*) from Rome's past therefore lined the hemicycles and porticoes.

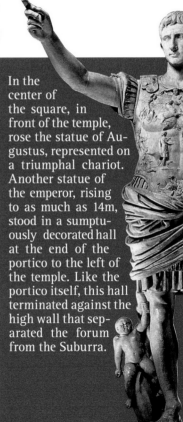

In the center of the square, in front of the temple, rose the statue of Augustus, represented on a triumphal chariot. Another statue of the emperor, rising to as much as 14m, stood in a sumptuously decorated hall at the end of the portico to the left of the temple. Like the portico itself, this hall terminated against the high wall that separated the forum from the Suburra.

Portrait statue of the emperor Augustus found at Prima → Porta to the north of Rome (Vatican Museum).

···THE PALATINE

Palatine, Domus Augustana: internal ↑ court with fountain and motif of four «*peltae*» (the shields of the Amazons).

The Domus Augustana, → reconstruction of the central area.

(→ For the Romans, **the Palatine** had always represented the city's sacred birthplace. All ancient authors agree with the archeological evidence that the hill, isolated from the others and in a position which dominated both the Tiber, right by the Tiber Island, and also the Forum Boarium market, was the site of the legendary 'founding' of Rome and the 'square furrow' ploughed by Romulus on 21 April of the year 754/3 BC. Legend apart, the hill has disclosed the remains of early bronze-age huts, providing incontrovertible evidence of the presence of an inhabited area in the very place to which ancient tradition ascribed the *casa Romuli*, ie the hut of the legendary founder. This was certainly one and probably also the most important of the villages from which the city of Rome was to evolve over the course of time.

The history of the Palatine is rather obscure during the early centuries of the city's existence and, apart from **Temples of Victory, of Jupiter Stator, of Jupiter Victor** and of the **Magna Mater**, no public buildings were erected there.

← Painting from the «House of Livia» on the Palatine.

→ Painting showing Apollo Citharoedus (Augustan age, Antiquarium of the Palatine).

(→ On the other hand, many private homes and 'urban' villas were built there by the rich and famous, especially during the last two centuries of the Republic.

In 44 BC Augustus too decided to transfer his home there, where he also ordered the building of a temple dedicated to Apollo, inaugurated in 28 BC. From then on almost all the emperors went to live on the Palatine, which was gradually transformed into a single, sumptuous royal residence, the archetypal 'palace', a term which derives from the name of the hill, the *Palatium*.

The first true imperial palace was the work of Tiberius, successor of Augustus. He was followed by Caligula, who extended the building as far as the edge of the cliff overlooking the forum, while Claudius and Nero (between 41 and 60 AD) built the so-called **Domus Transitoria**, which soon burnt down in the great Neronian fire of 64 and was never rebuilt. It was Domitian who built a new palace on the ruins and, by occupying also the areas left free by his predecessors, created a new, more grandiose palace. Domitian's complex, known as the **Domus Augustana**, or House of Augustus (i.e. of the Emperor), consisted basically of a public palace and a private residence, a large stadium or hippodrome, and baths.

Statue of a Nymph (?) of the end of the → Iˢᵗ century AD from the Stadium of the Palatine.

Statue of Satyr, → 2ⁿᵈ century AD (*Antiquarium* of the Palatine).

(→ Extending along the slopes of the hill and up to the summit, with halls and stairways, rooms and peristyles, porticoes, terraces and fountains, the great *domus* was, to put it in the words of the poet Martial, 'one of the most beautiful things in the world, a tall and massive pile composed of seven hills placed one on top of the other, until they touch the sky'. Septimius Severus, who reigned at the turn of the second and third centuries, artificially extended the level of the hill southwards as far as the stands of the Circus Maximus below, carried on a series of brickwork arcades in two orders, rising to a height of 20-30m. Right at the bottom of the hill, Severus also erected the famous **Septizodium**, a remarkable multistorey structure, richly adorned with columns, niches and statues and probably animated by the play of running water like a nymphaeum, to greet the eye and invite the admiration of the traveler as

The Stadium of the Palatine, → reconstruction.

he entered Rome by the Via Appia. After Septimius Severus there were no more important works on the Palatine except a temple built by Elagabalus, in the 3rd century AD, in a corner opposite the Colosseum. Rather, starting with Diocletian at the beginning of the 4th century, the emperors actually began to desert it. This abandonment became definitive when Constantine transferred the capital of the empire to Byzantium.

63

(→ In 64 AD most of the center of Rome was destroyed in an enormous fire which started in the area of the Circus Maximus and reached the top of the Esquiline. While the story blaming Nero for the fire gained currency as a result of the emperor's already bad reputation, the destruction wrought by the disaster certainly made it easier to construct the most extensive *domus* ever built, awarded the epithet *aurea* for the magnificence of its decoration and the opulence of its buildings.

The architects engaged for the building of the palace, *Severus* and *Celer*, decided to adopt the format of a country villa right in the center of Rome, and the 2nd century historian Tacitus notes that the *domus* was admired by people at the time not so much for its precious materials, already seen in the previ-

ous palace, as for its woods, pastures and lakes, the largest of which filled the site now occupied by the Colosseum.

The buildings therefore covered a vast area extending from the Palatine to the Oppian, at the foot of the Celian.

Domus Aurea, reconstruction of the octagonal hall. →

THE DOMUS AUREA ...

Domus Aurea, painting with the → representation of Achilles among King Lycomedes' daughters, in the palace of Scyros.

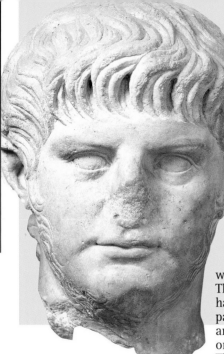

↑ Head portrait of emperor Nero
(Rome, National Museum).

■
■
■

Domus Aurea, niche with a ↗
painted false window.

(→ Suetonius, author of the biographies of the first twelve Caesars, recounts that the *atrium* of the palace consisted of a triple portico which was a thousand paces long (about 1,500 meters) and contained the Colossus, a statue of Nero 120 feet high (35 meters).

The decoration of the interiors made use of all kinds of precious materials: gold and ivory were everywhere, and the flowers in the paintings were set with precious stones. The ceilings of the banqueting halls were fitted with sliding panels of ivory, so that flowers and perfumes could be scattered onto the diners from above.

The pictorial decoration, entrusted to the painter *Fabullus*, was in an opulent, magnificent style, depicting figures framed in geometric patterns which were endlessly enriched by the motifs of plants and imaginary creatures. It is the Oppian Hill sector of this imposing residence that we know best. Built on platforms overlooking the valley in which the Colosseum was later to rise, it was divided into three main blocks.

The two lateral ones were based on the traditional nucleus of the peristyle villa, their rooms distributed around a porticoed garden.

↑ Domus Aurea, flying figures in the vault of the room of Hector and Andromache.

(→ The central block, separated from the others by large pentagonal gardens, was, on the other hand, built around an octagonal hall, the vault of which was supported by octagonal pillars, with a circular light-well in the center. The sides of the octagon gave onto rectangular rooms, which all looked back towards the center of the hall, where a statue was probably placed, lit to striking effect from the light well above. This was certainly one of the banqueting halls of the *domus*, perhaps the main one which – Suetonius recounts – rotated continuously on its own axis, like the earth.

After Nero's death in 68 AD, the emperors who succeeded him returned large parts of the Domus Aurea to the city. Thus, on top of Nero's palace, rose public monuments like the Colosseum and all the buildings connected with it (e.g. the gladiators' barracks, their hospital and the depot for the stage equipment used during the spectacles), the public baths built by Titus and also the state mint (*Moneta*). The last sector to be dismantled was the luxurious Oppian Hill area which, having been stripped of all its recyclable materials, was interred for the construction of the Baths of Trajan.

THE CIRCUS MAXIMUS

The circus and the spectators (Tunis, Museum of Bardo)

(→ Tradition had it that the first circus on this site was built by King Tarquinius Priscus to mark the place where the rape of the Sabine women had been perpetrated. However this may be, the **Circus Maximus** was used for chariot racing and can be considered as the largest building ever put up for entertainment purposes. Indeed, when the *circus* attained its greatest size, in the heyday of the imperial age, it measured no less than 600m in length and 200m in width, and could accommodate up to 300,000 spectators. The last of the major reconstructions of the *circus* was undertaken by Trajan at the beginning of the 2nd century AD, though it was later enlarged by Caracalla and restored by Constantine, while Constans, as late as 357 AD, had it adorned with an Egyptian obelisk (attributed to Thutmosis III), which thus came to make a pair with the one (bearing the cartouche of Ramses II) that Augustus had erected at the center of the *spina*, the characteristic barrier that ran down the middle of the arena, thus defining the circuit that the chariots had to complete seven times before reaching the finishing line. The seating area was divided into three sections by horizontal gangways, interrupted on Palatine side by the great imperial 'box', which was in direct communication with the palaces on the top of the hill. But a part of the seating, presumably the topmost rows, must have been sustained by wooden structures, because the records apprise us of frequent collapses: one such disaster killed 1,112 spectators in the time of Antoninus Pius and another, under

The Circus Maximus, reconstruction. →

Diocletian, no less than 13,000. The Circus Maximus had a long life. Races were still being organized there in the 5th century AD, the last spectacle to be put on being the one sponsored by Totila, King of the Ostrogoths, in 549. The two obelisks were unearthed in 1588 and Pope Sixtus V had them removed and re-erected, one in Piazza del Popolo and the other in front of the side entrance of St John in Lateran, where they can still be seen today.

↑ Mosaic with horses and grooms; the horses represent the four rival factions of the circus (Sousse-Tunisia).

↓↘↘ Mosaics representing *aurigae* (chariot drivers) from the Roman villa of Baccano (3rd century AD).

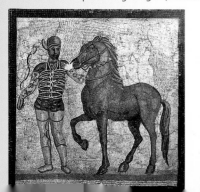

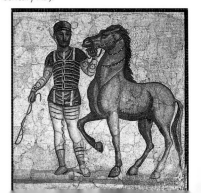

THE THEATER OF MARCELLUS

During the Republic, the censors forbade the construction of permanent theaters, this in deference to the puritan spirit of traditional Roman custom, which saw in theatrical spectacles a danger to public morality: the only theaters permitted were of wood. It was not until the last years of the Republic that Pompey dared to put up the first theater built of stone. Pompey's theater was followed by the Theater of Balbus and the Theater of Marcellus, which occupies a site between the Capitol and the Tiber and is the only one that can still be seen today. It was begun by Caesar and completed by Augustus in 11 BC, when he dedicated it to the memory of his nephew and heir Marcellus.

The theater had a diameter of 130m, rose to a height of 30m, and could seat about 15,000 spectators.

Head of Theseus from the pediment of the Temple of Apollo Sosianus. →

(→ In the Middle Ages it was used as a fortress by the noble Roman families, and in the 16th century it was transformed into a palace for the Caetani by the architect Baldassare Peruzzi.

The choice of this site for the theater had been determined by that of the adjoining **Temple of Apollo**, where, already in Republican times, the special games celebrated in honour of the god included theatrical spectacles. The original temple was founded in 431 BC, when the cult of Apollo *medicus* (Apollo the healer) was introduced to Rome for the first time as the result of a vow made during a grave outbreak of pestilence. What can be seen today, however, goes back to a radical reconstruction undertaken by the Consul Gaius Sosius in 36 BC. Finely decorated with reliefs and sculptures, the Sosian Temple, as Romans dubbed it, incorporated in the triangular space of its pediment an original Greek sculpture that

The Theater of Marcellus, the → Temple of Apollo Sosianus and, on the right, the Temple of Bellona.

← Columns of the Temple of Apollo Sosianus.

went back to the 5th century BC and depicted a battle between Amazons.

The slightly smaller temple by the side of the Temple of Apollo cannot be attributed with certainty, though there are reasons for thinking that it might be the one that Appius Claudius Caecus, builder of the Via Appia, dedicated to Bellona in 296 BC.

THE THEATER OF MARCELLUS

← The Propylaeum (entrance gateways) of the Portico of Octavia, dedicated to Augustus's sister in 23 BC. The remains visible today, behind the Marcellus Theater, belong to a restoration carried out under emperor Septimius Severus after a fire (191 AD). In the 8th century AD the Propylaeum were incorporated into the façade of the present church of S. Angelo in Peschiera and surrounded by the fish market (*Forum Piscium*). Pope Paul IV in 1555 with his papal bull «*Cum nimis absurdum*» revoked all the rights of the Jewish community of Rome and imposed that the area around the Portico of Ottavia be considered thereon as a «Ghetto».

THE PANTHEON

Portrait of Agrippa, Augustus's friend and son-in-law, →
who erected the first Pantheon.

A splendid temple in honour of all the Olympian gods was erected in the Campus Martius by Marcus Vipsanius Agrippa, son-in-law and counselor of the Emperor Augustus, between 27 and 25 AD. The temple therefore became known as the **Pantheon**, a Greek name meaning 'of all the Gods'. What we see today, however, preserved substantially just as it was in antiquity, is not Agrippa's original temple, but rather the result of a complete reconstruction undertaken by Hadrian between 118 and 125 AD, the first temple having been destroyed by fire in 80 AD. Wholly different from its predecessor, the new Pantheon had a great circular hall roofed by a hemispherical vault with an opening at the center, 9m in diameter. The diameter of the hall (and therefore also of the dome) stretches 43.3m and is exactly equal to the greatest height of the building, so that its interior could accommodate a perfect sphere of that diameter. The entrance to the rotunda from the outside is through a traditional pronaos with sixteen monolithic columns of Egyptian granite arranged in two orders of eight columns each. The inscription in bronze letters on the architrave (the bronze is modern but set in the original cuttings) records the temple's foundation by Agrippa in his third consulate. The pediment above the architrave was decorated with reliefs in gilt bronze, and the internal trabeation of the pronaos was originally lined with the same material. The bronze was removed by Pope Urban VIII and then used by Bernini to cast the great baldacchino over the Confessione in St Peter's.

(→ Inside the Pantheon there are numerous other monolithic columns, great rarities, in Numidian yellow and Phrygian purple.

The interior survives in its original form, perfectly preserved, and in this respect it is unique among the monuments of antiquity. Pope Boniface IV received the building as a gift from the Byzantine emperor Phocas in 608 AD and transformed it from a pagan temple into a Christian church, dedicating it to the Madonna and all the martyrs (Santa Maria *ad Martyres*).

The interior of the Pantheon. →

The Pantheon, the façade and a→ section of the interior, reconstruction.

THE MAUSOLEUM OF HADRIAN

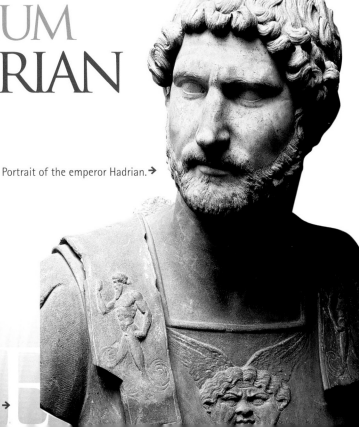

(→ Following the example of Augustus, who had built a Mausoleum in the Campus Martius, the emperor Hadrian (117-138 AD) decided to build a monumental tomb for himself and his successors during his lifetime. The resulting **Mausoleum of Hadrian** was erected on the right bank of the Tiber, not far from that of Augustus, in the area occupied by the gardens of the family of the Domitii, near the edge of the Vatican Fields. Begun around 130 AD, it had a massive cylindrical core, 64m in diameter, the lower part of which was surrounded by a square base completely veneered in marble.

Portrait of the emperor Hadrian. →

The Mausoleum of Hadrian, reconstruction. →

(→ An earthen tumulus probably rose above this cylinder, the monument being crowned by a huge central pillar surmounted by a gilt bronze statue of the emperor in a chariot. The building was incomplete when Hadrian died and he could not be buried there until a year later, in 139 AD, after Antoninus Pius had finished the great tomb. To facilitate direct access to the tomb from the Campus Martius, Hadrian also built the bridge to which he gave his family name, the *Pons Aelius*, a greater and more elaborate structure than any of its predecessors. It survived intact until the end of the last century, though by that time known as **Ponte Sant'Angelo**, but then had to be interfered with to permit construction of the modern Tiber embankments; the two end spans were in fact rebuilt at that time, so that only the three central arches now survive as they were originally built between 130 and 134 AD.

The Mausoleum was included by Honorius, at the beginning of the 5th century, in the defensive system of the Aurelian Walls, as a kind of outlying bastion, and perhaps from the 10th century onwards, it was transformed into a fortress, **Castel Sant'Angelo**, serving to defend the Vatican, to which it was linked by a special 'viaduct' (raised passageway).

← Castel Sant'Angelo, night view.

THE STADIUM ···
OF DOMITIAN
(PIAZZA NAVONA)

(→ The stadium was built by emperor Domitian around 85 AD on the edge of the central part of the Campus Martius, where most probably already Caesar, in 46 BC and Augustus in 28 BC had raised similar facilities but provisory and built of wood. Domitian reserved it for athletic games which, together with musical and poetic competitions that were held in the nearby Odeon that he had built southwards from the stadium, were part of the *Certamen Capitolinum* (games in honour of Jupiter Capitolinus), instituted in 86 AD.

The stadium, inspired by Greek models, extended for a length of 275 m with a width of 106m and could hold 30.000 spectators. It must have had a grandiose appearance seen from outside with two orders of superimposed arches supported by travertine pilasters, decorated with Ionic columns (and maybe Corinthian in the second order): behind the arches, at ground level ran three parallel corridors, with radial walls which supported the cavea and the stairways that led up to the tiers of seats divided into two sectors, one above the other (*moeniana*). One of the shorter sides, the northern one, was curved and had at its center an entryway preceded by a portico with two marble columns, while other two entryways where placed on the two long sides of the building. It is quite probable that there was a fourth entryway, on the southern short side.

↑ Marble portrait of emperor Domitian.

↑ Piazza Navona: detail of the fountain of the 4 Rivers and church of St Agnese in Agone.

the ancient track or arena of the stadium while the surrounding buildings were built on the site of the seat tiers on which they are founded; remains of the pre-existing roman structures are still visible below the street level on the short northern side as well as in the cellars of some of the buildings and beneath the church of St Agnese in Agone.

← Remains of structures belonging to the Stadium of Domitian visible in Piazza di Tor Sanguigna.

(→ The stadium was restored by the emperor Alexander Severus in 228 AD and was used up to the early Vth century. Afterwards it was progressively demolished to reuse its materials, in its place was built, during the Renaissance a piazza which exactly followed its plan and dimensions, saving the same curve of its northern side. The name «Navona» probably comes from the athletic games (*agones*) which took place in the area; the latin term «*in agone*» in time was transformed into the vulgar «nagone» and then into the final name of «navona». In particular piazza Navona extends over the area of

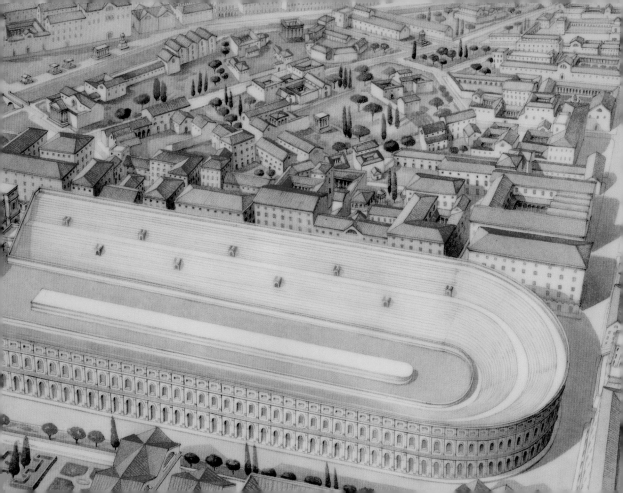

THE SACRED AREA OF LARGO ARGENTINA

Largo Argentina, reconstruction of →
Temples A and B.

(→ The archaeological complex known as the «Sacred Area» of Largo Argentina was discovered totally by chance during the summer of 1926, during demolition work that was being carried out in the neighborhood.

The southern area of the Campus Martius in which the buildings stand is delimited to the north by the *Hecatostylum* (the «portico of the 100 columns»); to the south by the buildings adjoining the Circus Flaminius; to the west by the Portico and Theater of Pompey; to the east, by a large porticoed square (the *Porticus Minucia Frumentaria*). The «Sacred Area» contains four Republican Age temples, commonly indicated with the first four letters of the alphabet; the buildings feature various chronological phases showing a succession of changes made to them over time. We can recognize three levels: the original one to which the oldest temples belong, followed by a late Republican tuff pavement and an Imperial age travertine pavement. The oldest temple of the cultural complex is **Temple C**, which, on the basis of the construction technique and fragments of architectural decoration, has been dated to the early 3rd century BC.

← Colossal statue of a female divinity from Temple B (Rome, Capitoline Museum).

(→ **Temple A** stands on the northern side of the area and its first phase can also be dated to the 3rd century BC, although it underwent radical changes down through the centuries. Its current appearance probably dates to the period of Pompey, around the mid 1st century BC. It is a peripteral temple, with tuff columns and travertine capitals. However, the travertine columns that are now visible belong to a later restoration date. **Temple D**, the largest, situated near the southern extremity of the area, also currently stands in its rebuilt state, completely in travertine, dating from the late Republican Age, while the oldest phase probably dates from the early 2nd century BC.

The last temple, chronologically speaking, is **Temple B**, a circular building on a podium, with a staircase at the front, tuff Corinthian columns, and travertine capitals. Parts of the cult statue, a colossal goddess carved out of Greek marble, have been found near the building: it was an acrolith, and the garment parts were probably made of metal (today it is kept in the Capitoline Museums).

It is very probable that Temple B can be identified with *Aedes Fortunae Huiusce Diei* (the «Fortune of the Present Day»), founded in 101 BC by consul Quintus Lutatius Catulus, together with Marius, to commemorate the battle of Vercelli against the Cimbri. For Temple C, a probable attribution is to Feronia, an Italic goddess who had, in ancient times, a temple in the Campus Martius.

The attribution of Temple A appears more problematic; a passage from Ovid seems to indicate that it may have been dedicated to Juturna, a goddess of wells and springs. The temple was probably the religious center of ancient Rome's Water Office (the *Statio aquarum*).

Largo Argentina, structures of Temple A. →

The Tiber Island with the remains of the Aemilian Bridge (the so-called «Ponte Rotto»). ↑

THE TIBER ISLAND

(→ According to ancient tradition, **the Tiber Island** was formed after the expulsion of the last king, Tarquin the Proud, when the people threw into the river the sheaves of wheat belonging to the fugitive king, which they had looted from the Campus Martius. In actual fact, however, the island must have developed by natural means at a point where the river broadened and the strength of its currents became very weak and, what is more, long before the Romans chased out the Tarquins. The island was of very great importance in the archaic period because it facilitated the crossing of the river and thus ensured continuity in the lines of communication that linked the Tyrrhenian seaboard to the north of the river with its counterpart to the south.

The island was therefore a strategic point and, as such, was one of the causes that brought the city of Rome into being. A great embankment wall built round the island gave it the appearance of a boat, and a small obelisk erected in the centre, suggesting a mast, further enhanced this effect. In 291 BC a **Temple of Aesculapius** was established there in the aftermath of a grave pestilence and from that time onwards the island acquired a sacred character connected essentially with health practices and the cult of the god of medicine. The temple was surrounded by porticoes which provided shelter for the sick pilgrims who came to be cured. It is noteworthy that the island has retained this function up to the present day, with the presence of a modern hospital (run, what is more, by a religious order).

Towards the end of the Republic the island was linked to the land by two bridges. The *Pons Fabricius*, leading to the left bank, was constructed in 62 BC, probably to replace an earlier wooden structure, and it is still completely preserved. The *Pons Cestius*, which leads to the right bank and the area of Trastevere (beyond the Tiber), was put up shortly after, in 46 BC, but then wholly rebuilt by the Emperors Valentinian I, Valens and Gratian in 370 AD. Unfortunately, however, even this bridge was completely reconstructed towards the end of last century.

The Tiber Island with the Temple ➔
of Aesculapius, reconstruction.

← The serpent of Aesculapius, god of medecine, swimming to the Tiber Island.

St Peter's Basilica, general view. →

ST PETER

(→ On the 23rd of December in the Holy Year 1950 pope Pius XII announced to the world, that the excavations carried out beneath the crypt under the High Altar of the Vatican basilica had rediscovered the tomb of St Peter. A cloud of uncertainty which for some time had been growing more dense and which no one had ever before dared face could at last be said to have been dispersed. But the remarkable discovery was only the confirmation of a tradition which for almost two thousand years had revered the spot beneath the papal altar as the grave of the prince of Apostles in spite of the attempts to deny not only that Peter died and was buried at Rome, but also that he ever came to the Eternal City.

In actual fact the astonishing chain of events concerning the fisherman of Galilee who, after receiving from Christ the mission of building the Church came to Rome, the centre of the empire to make it, with his blood, the centre of the Church itself, has remained completely , and perhaps for ever, wrapped in uncertainty: there is no reliable testimony of the year of his arrival in Rome, the time of his stay is obscure, and even the year of his martyrdom is uncertain.

We have only legend and religious tradition, which deal principally with the last «acts» of the apostle's life on earth.

The most memorable part of the tradition is that which recounts Christ's miraculous appearance before St Peter on the Via Appia while he was hurriedly leaving Rome, pursued by the Neronian persecution.

The account has come down to us both of how the astonished Peter turned towards his Master and asked: «*Domine, quo vadis?*» («Lord, where goest thou?») and of how Christ replied sadly: «*Venio iterum crucifigi*» («I come to be crucified a second time»). This, it is said, caused St Peter's noble change of heart: he decided to return to the City, ready to face there the supreme sacrifice. On the spot marked out by the tra-dition, by the junction of the Appia and the Ardeatina there is still a small church dating from the ninth century (rebuilt, however, in the early years of the seventeenth century) with the exact name «*Quo vadis?*».

The other stories all concern the imprisonment of Peter as well as that of Paul in the Mamertine goal.

The chains that were said to have tied Peter are kept as relics in the basilica of San Pietro in Vincoli, on the Esquiline hill where they were already saved since the 5th century. Compared with so many legends the reliable evidence as regards the martyrdom and subsequent burial is extensive.

As for the place of his martyrdom, the sources all agree in situating it on the slopes of the Vatican hill not very far from the circus built by Caligula (37-41), later completed by Nero (54-68), *iuxta obeliscum* (that is next to the obelisk, which was the most distinctive «monument» in the circus). According to tradition, it was here that innumerable Christians were killed amid atrocious ordeals, accused by Nero of having caused the disastrous fire of Rome in 64 AD.

← Bronze statue of St Peter.

Vatican Necropolis, ↑
Julian mausoleum:
mosaic with portrayal
of Christ as the Rising Sun.

(→ These included the Apostle Peter, who was buried on the north-west slope of the Vatican Hill in a necropolis which extended along a small, secondary cemetery road (parallel to the eastern long-side of the circus), in a sector reserved for the poor, surrounded by other pagan tombs. This road was also lined by various mausoleums, built from the 2nd century onwards, some of which show signs of having also been occupied by Christian tombs at a later time. Of all the various inscriptions which have been preserved, mention should be made of that of Mausoleum H, which beseeches Peter «to pray to Christ for the holy Christians buried at his threshold». Many of these mausoleums are decorated by paintings, stucco-work and mosaics, and often contain sarcophagi. The most representative on this site is Mausoleum M, built in the early 3rd century AD, the vault of which contains a decoration in mosaic in which Christ is portrayed, like Apollo, on the Chariot of the Sun. The **Tomb of Peter** is located at the western end of the necropolis, and it has undergone radical modifications over the centuries due to the deep veneration of which the Apostle has always been object. Originally, it took the form of a tomb dug out of the bare earth, perhaps with a covering composed of a double row of leaning tiles placed over the body. Around the mid-2nd century AD a wall dressed with red plaster was built to protect the tomb of Peter from becoming covered with earth deposits from the hill above. The wall was interrupted at the point corresponding to the tomb by an aedicule with two niches, one above the other, hollowed out in the wall itself and divided lengthwise by a slab of travertine supported by two small marble columns. It was the first monument to be built over the tomb of the Apostle. Around it have been found the remains of many fairly simple burials dating from the 2nd-4th centuries, i.e. when the mausoleums of the necropolis also started to be occupied by Christians.

St Peter, reconstruction of the nave of Constantine's basilica. →

THE BASILICA OF CONSTANTINE

(→ In the early years of the 4th century, Constantine (306-337) ordered the levelling of the slope of the hill on which the necropolis had developed, with the result that it was covered over. On top, he ordered the construction of a grandiose basilica in honour of the Prince of the Apostles.

Consecrated by pope Silvester on the 18th November 326 AD the great church of Constantine (begun in 324 and finished only in 349) covered part of the northern sector of the circus of Caligula and Nero and part of the necropolis besides, leaving intact the tomb of Peter. The monument, which measured 85 meters by 64, was of a nave and four aisles, with transept and apse. The façade was preceded by a vast atrium with a rectangular portico and a fountain for ablutions in the center (*cantharus*).

At the point at which the transept intersected with the nave, exactly over the Tomb of St Peter, the emperor Constantine and his mother Helena erected a monument which was splendid in its simplicity: a marble caisson-like structure decorated with a golden cross and covered by a *pergula* sustained by vine-covered

St Peter and reconstruction of the façade of →
Constantine's basilica.

spiralled columns that are still saved: they were re-used by Bernini to decorate, in the present Basilica, the loggia of the four enormous pilasters which sustain the cupola. At the center of the *pergula* there must of hung an imperial crown, at the same time a symbolic ornament and the place from which were suspended the lamps that illuminated the celebrations. The crown in fact hung not over the marble case, but over a free space right in front of it where, during mass, a mobile altar was placed.

It was only with Gregory the Great (592-604) that the basilica had a fixed altar, over the constantinian marble memory, which was enclosed in a semi-circular corridor. The altar of Gregory the Great was later en-globed within those of Callistus II and Clement VIII.

It is recorded that Charlemagne was crowned in this church by Leo III on Christmas Day of the year 800. At the height of the Middle Ages, the number of facilities in the surrounding area gradually increased, catering to the needs of the crowds of pilgrims who massed here from every corner of the world to venerate the tomb of the Apostle and those of the other Roman martyrs.

In 846 the basilica was sacked by the Saracens. Following this disastrous event, Leo IV (847-855) built a defensive wall around the entire neighbourhood around the church, which had until then lain outside the Aurelian walls, being on the other side of the river. Thus a fortified citadel was created: the *Civitas Leoniana.*

During the 13th century the complex consolidated its double function of citadel and place of residence of the Bishop of Rome as an alternative to the Lateran Palace. Rooms were added (including the Palatine Chapel, on the site of the later Sistine Chapel), along with loggias and gardens, and the site was linked to Castel Sant'Angelo by means of a covered walkway built on top of the walls.

Several times restored and enlarged, about one thousand years after its erection the basilica was threatening to fall in ruins, and pope Nicholas V entrusted Bernardo Rossellino with restoring it but the Pope died in 1455 and all work was suspended until the year 1506 when pope Julius II ordered the basilica's total reconstruction and entrusted it to Bramante, who thought of rebuilding it by «erecting the Pantheon upon the basilica of Constantine».

THE BASILICA OF MICHELANGELO

(→ On 18 April 1506, Bramante embarked upon a reconstruction of the church which was to dispense completely with Constantine's edifice, now in serious disrepair, and also on the construction of the Vatican Palace. The work proceeded with the gradual demolition of the old basilica, as the construction of the new one went ahead. Work for the enormous new construction lasted more than one hundred years, through alterations, changes of plan, additions and modifications, under the guidance of famous architects as, after Bramante, Raphael, Giuliano da Sangallo, Baldassare Peruzzi, Antonio da Sangallo the younger, Michelangelo, Vignola, Giacomo della Porta, Domenico Fontana, Carlo Maderno and Bernini.

The definitive design was that of Michelangelo: the new church was to be in the form of a Greek cross, with a nave and four aisles, bigger than the old one but smaller than the one designed by Bramante, and its focal point was the dome which would rise over the tomb of Peter. By the first quarter of the 17th century, the building work had been substantially completed, with further modifications to the initial plans: the dome was vaulted, the obe-

The dome of Michelangelo. →

← Chair of St Peter, in gilded bronze.

lisk previously situated in the middle of the *spina* of the Circus of Caligula was transferred to its present position and, most importantly, Paul V (1605-1621) had reverted to the idea of a basilica in the shape of the Latin cross. Maderno therefore elongated the edifice with the addition of three chapels on each side, increasing it to its present size, and he also erected the façade, which was completed in 1614.

The result was the superb largest church of Christianity, consecrated by pope Urban VIII on the 18th of November 1626, one thousand three hundred years after the first consecration. In the center of the basilica, under Michelangelo's magnificent dome, which rises to a height of 394 ft, the papal altar represents the heart and pivot both of the basilica itself and of Christian Rome, in so far it rises exactly over the place where St Peter was buried. The interior decoration was provided by Bernini, in the Baroque style. Alexander VII (1655-1667) was responsible for the large, colonnaded piazza which, with its two semi-circular arms, originally connected the basilica to the neighbourhoods of Borgo Vecchio and Borgo Nuovo. Ideologically, the piazza represented the last of the Imperial Fora, the «Foro Cristiano».

← Michelangelo's Pietà, detail.

The interior of the basilica of St Peter is of grandiose dimensions and full of works of art. Among the most important are: the **bronze baldacchino** above the altar, by Bernini, with its twisted columns reproducing those of the 6th century *ciborium*; the **Chair of St Peter**, also by Bernini, in gilded bronze, enclosing the ancient papal chair, of wood, inlaid with ivory decorations; some of the popes' funerary monuments; the **bronze statue of St Peter**, believed to be a 5th century work, in reality of the 13th century, the object of such daily veneration by the faithful that its feet have been worn down; and the **Pietà**, the famous marble group executed by Michelangelo in 1498-99 at the age of twenty-three, the only work to which the artist ever put his name. In addition, the lengths of the biggest churches in the world are marked on the floor, albeit with a few errors, down the middle line of the nave as measured from the apse. **The Sacred Vatican Grottoes** extend underneath the nave of the church. These contain the tombs of many popes and rulers, many early Christian sarcophagi and various pieces of architectural decoration originating from Constantine's church.

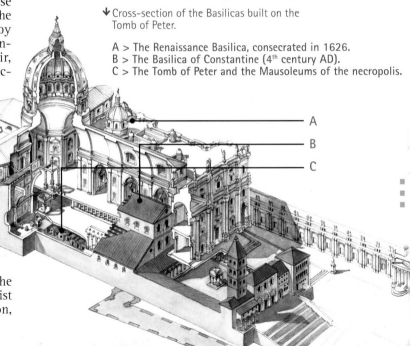

↓ Cross-section of the Basilicas built on the Tomb of Peter.

A > The Renaissance Basilica, consecrated in 1626.
B > The Basilica of Constantine (4th century AD).
C > The Tomb of Peter and the Mausoleums of the necropolis.

A

B

C

THE SISTINE CHAPEL
"SO GOD CREATED MAN"

(→ The Sistine Chapel is the heart of the Vatican Palaces which lie at the side of the great basilica of St Peter's and have been the papal residence since 1377.

Built in 1437 by pope Sixtus IV, it is the most famous hall in the world, because of the magnificent frescoes by Michelangelo – of the

Last Judgement on the far wall, and for the Creation and other Old Testament stories on the ceiling. The focal point of this is the amazing Creation of Man – that creature whom God made ruler of the Universe and for whose redemption He sent His Son incarnate into the world, whose first vicar was, through divine ordinance, the disciple and apostle Peter.

A Sistine Chapel, the Creation of Man.

B Sistine Chapel, the Last Judgement: Christ Judging.

C Sistine Chapel, the Last Judgement: one of the Damned.

D Sistine Chapel, vault: the «Delphic Sybil».